About the Author

Born in Germany, Edgar Rothermich studied music and sound er[...] prestigious Tonmeister program at the Berlin Institute of Technology (TU) and the University of Arts (UdK) in Berlin where he graduated in 1989 with a Master's Degree. He worked as a composer and music producer in Berlin, and moved to Los Angeles in 1991 where he continued his work on numerous projects in the music and film industry ("The Celestine Prophecy", "Outer Limits", "Babylon 5", "What the Bleep Do We Know", "Fuel", "Big Money Rustlas").

For over 20 years, Edgar has had a successful musical partnership with electronic music pioneer and founding Tangerine Dream member Christopher Franke. In addition to his collaboration with Christopher, Edgar has been working with other artists, as well as on his own projects.

In 2010 he started to release his solo records in the "Why Not …" series with different styles and genres. The current releases are "Why Not Solo Piano", "Why Not Electronica", "Why Not Electronica Again", and "Why Not 90s Electronica". This previously unreleased album was produced in 1991/1992 by Christopher Franke. All albums are available on Amazon and iTunes, including the 2012 release, the re-recording of the Blade Runner Soundtrack.

In addition to composing music, Edgar Rothermich is writing technical manuals with a unique style, focusing on rich graphics and diagrams to explain concepts and functionality of software applications under his popular GEM series (Graphically Enhanced Manuals). His best-selling titles are available as printed books on Amazon, as Multi-Touch eBooks on the iBooks Store, and as pdf downloads from his website.

Since 2017, Edgar Rothermich is Adjunct Professor at the Fullerton College Fine Arts Department, teaching Electronic Music, Synthesis, Audio Production, Pro Tools, and Logic Pro.

www.DingDingMusic.com   GEM@DingDingMusic.com

● *Special Thanks*

Special thanks to my beautiful wife, Li, for her love, support, and understanding during those long hours of working on the books. And not to forget my son, Winston. Waiting for him during soccer practice or Chinese class always gives me extra time to work on a few chapters.

The manual is based on VCV Rack v0.6.2c
Manual: Print Version 2018-1218
ISBN-13: 978-1791965693

🟡 *About the GEM (Graphically Enhanced Manuals)*

UNDERSTAND, not just LEARN

What are Graphically Enhanced Manuals? They're a new type of manual with a visual approach that helps you UNDERSTAND a program, not just LEARN it. No need to read through 500 pages of dry text explanations. Rich graphics and diagrams help you to get that "aha" effect and make it easy to comprehend difficult concepts. The Graphically Enhanced Manuals help you master a program much faster with a much deeper understanding of concepts, features, and workflows in a very intuitive way that is easy to understand.

All titles are available in three different formats:

.... pdf downloads from my website www.DingDingMusic.com/Manuals

.... multi-touch iBooks on Apple's iBooks Store

.... printed books on Amazon.com

(some manuals are also available in Deutsch, Español, 简体中文)

For a list of all the available titles and bundles: www.DingDingMusic.com/Manuals
To be notified about new releases and updates, subscribe to subscribe@DingDingMusic.com

🟡 *About the Formatting*

I use a specific color code in my books:

Green colored text indicates keyboard shortcuts. I use the following abbreviations: **sh** (shift key), **ctr** (control key), **opt** (option key), **cmd** (command key). A plus (+) between the keys means that you have to press all those keys at the same time.

sh+opt+K means: Hold the shift and the option key while pressing the K key.

Blue colored text indicates an action with the mouse (click, double-click, drag, etc.) plus any modifier keys that need to be pressed down during that action. For example, *opt+drag*

Brown colored text indicates Menu Commands with a greater sign (➤) indicating submenus.

Edit ➤ Source Media ➤ All means "Click on the Edit Menu, scroll down to Source Media, and select the submenu All.

Dimmed Blue text indicates an important term.

Condensed text indicates a command or a label.

Blue arrows indicate what happens if you click on an item or popup menu •➔

Table of Contents

Software Installation

 Home Page

The download files for RACK are available on their website
https://vcvrack.com

 Download and Install the Rack Software

Use the following steps to download and install the software on macOS:

- ☑ ***Click*** the big button indicating macOS ❶
- ☑ This will download the file "**Rack-0.6.2c-mac.dmg**" ❷ to your **Download** folder.
- ☑ ***Double-click*** the file to open that disk image.
- ☑ It will open a Finder window ❸ with four files and three folder aliases.
- ☑ ***Drag*** the **Rack** ❹ file to the **Applications** ❺ folder, which will copy the Rack application to the **Applications** folder on your boot drive.
- ☑ To use the Rack app within your DAW (i.e. Logic Pro X), ***drag*** the file **VCV-Bridge.component** ❻ to the **Components** ❼ folder. This will copy the Plugin to the **Plugins** folder on your system drive.
- ☑ To use Rack with a DAW that uses the VST Plugin standard, ***drag*** the other two files **VCV-Bridge.vst** ❽ and **VCV-Bridge-fx.vst** ❾ to the **VST** ❿ folder in that window.

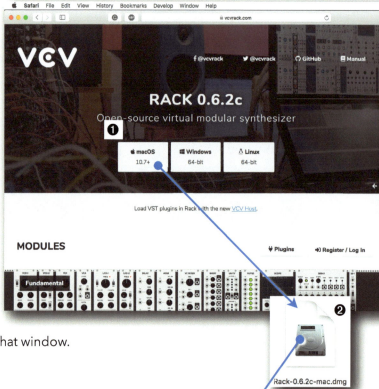

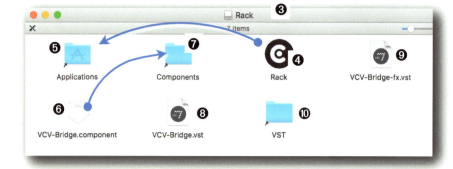

Create an Account

It is not necessary to create an account to use the basic version of Rack. However, if you want to download additional Modules, called Plugins (free or premium$), then you have to register and create a free account.

➡ Register

- ☑ **Register on the Website**: Go to the website http://vcvrack.com and *click* on the **Register/Log in ❶** button. This will open a window where you can provide your login credentials (email and password ❷). Then *click* the blue **Register ❸** button.

- ☑ **Register from the Rack software**: Once you have Rack installed and launched, you can also register directly from the app. *Click* on the **Register ❹** button, which opens your web browser with the vcvrack.com website where you register.

➡ Log in

- ☑ **Log in on the Website**: Go to the website http://vcvrack.com and *click* on the **Register/Log in ❶** button. This will open a window where you can provide your login credentials (email and password ❺). Then *click* the blue **Log in ❻** button.

- ☑ **Log in from the Rack software**: Once you have Rack installed and launched, you can also log in directly from the app. Enter your login credentials (email and password) in the two fields on the Toolbar on top ❼ and *click* the **Log in ❽** button next to it.

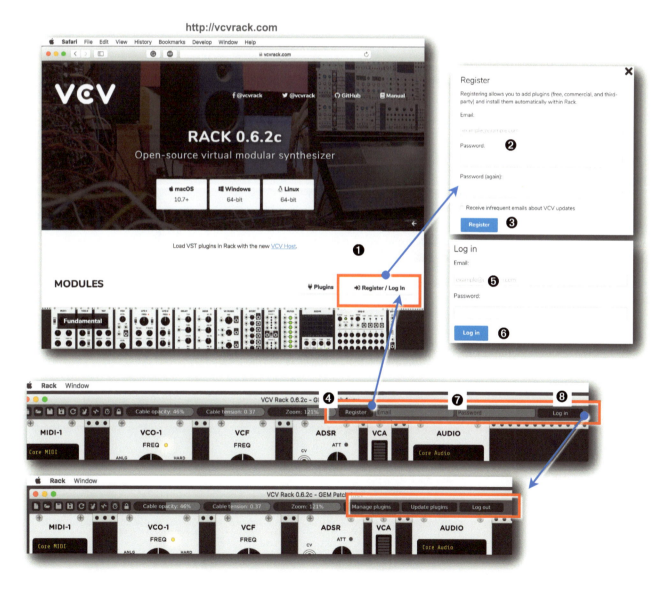

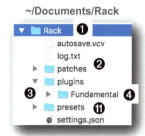

~/Documents/Rack

➡️ *Launch the Rack Software*

Go to the **Applications** folder on your boot drive and *double-click* the **Rack** application to launch the app.

When you launch the app the first time, it will create a new folder "**Rack**" ❶ in the user's Documents folder (*~/Documents/Rack/*) with three important subfolders inside, **patches** ❷, **plugins** ❸ and **presets** ⓫:

🟡 *plugins* ❸

This folder contains subfolders for each "author", which are the developers that created synth modules for this modular synth software. Inside each subfolder are the actual files that represent the individual modules.

The folder **Fundamental** ❹ contains the default modules that are installed with the software. The subfolder **res** ❺ contains svg files (*"Scalable Vector Graphics"* is an XML-based vector image format for two-dimensional graphics with support for interactivity and animating*), each one representing a specific module ❻.

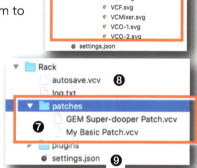

🟡 *patches* ❷

When you later save a patch that you created inside the Rack software, then that Patch will be stored as a Patch File ❼ placed in this **patches** folder, and that is the location from where you can later load Patches that you previously saved.

- ☑️ Patch Files have the **.vcv** file extension.
- ☑️ This is just the default location for the Patch Files, but you can save them to any other location on your drive.
- ☑️ You can easily exchange Patches with other users by exchanging those Patch Files, assuming that the other computer has the same Modules (plugins) installed.

🟡 *presets* ⓫

The **presets** folder contains Preset Files with the file extension .vcvm. These are the configurations for specific Modules that you can save as Preset Files.

🟡 *autosave.vcv*

The Rack software automatically saves any changes you make in your current Patch to that file **autosave.vcv** ❽. That means, if your software crashes or you close the app without saving your current Patch, it still will open the next time you launch the Rack software with all the changes you made.

🟡 *settings.jason*

The file **settings.jason** ❾ automatically stores any configuration settings that you make in the Rack software. For example, **Cable opacity**, **Cable tension**, and **Zoom** ❿.

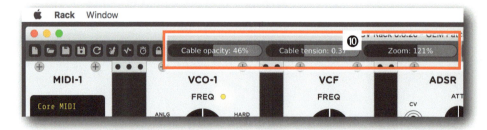

Install more Modules (Plugins)

Rack has a special procedure on how to get more Modules (called Plugins). It works based on a "relationship" between the VCV Rack website and your Rack software. This is something you first have to understand because you don't download Plugins directly from the website like you are used to with other software.

 Manage Plugins

In this first step, you only select which plugins you want to use. You are not actually downloading them from the website to your hard drive, you are only managing them on the website.

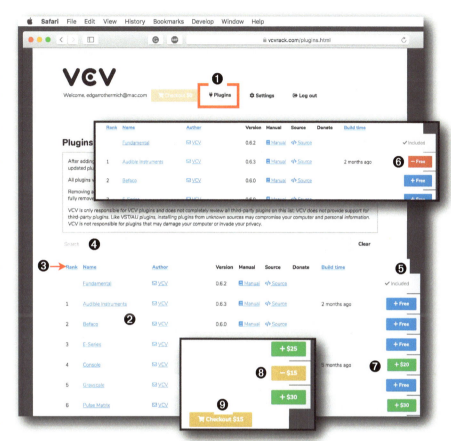

- ☑ All the available Plugins for the Rack software are available on the vcvrack.com website

- ☑ Go to vcvrack.com and *click* on the **Plugins ❶** button or go directly to the link https://vcvrack.com/plugins.html

- ☑ The Plugins page shows a list with 8 columns ❷, displaying all the available Plugins for the Rack software (over 100).

- ☑ **Sort List**: You can *click* on any active header ❸ to sort the Plugins list.

- ☑ **Search**: Enter a name in the **Search** field ❹ to search for a specific Plugin.

- ☑ **Name**: *Click* on a **Name** to open a window with more details about that Plugin, most likely a set of multiple Plugins.

- ☑ **Author**: The **Author** column indicates the developer of that Plugin with a link to their website and email link.

- ☑ **Manual**: The **Manual** link opens a page with instructions on how to use the Plugin(s).

- ☑ **Enable Button**: The buttons on the far right ❺ let you manage the Plugins:

> **+ Free**   All the free Plugins are indicated by this blue button. Just *click* on a button if you want to add it to your Rack software. Remember, this only marks that Plugin, it will not download it yet.

> **– Free**   Any Plugin that you selected will change its button to this red button ❻. That is an indication that it is part of your Plugin selection. *Click* on that button to remove it from your selection and it will turn blue again.

> **+ $15**   Any "non-free" Plugin has a green button ❼ indicating how much it costs. *Click* on the button to add it to your shopping cart.

> **– $15**   Once you selected a non-free Plugin, the green button turns yellow ❽ and a yellow **Checkout** button ❾ appears at the bottom of the page. You can either *click* on the plugin button again to remove it from the shopping cart or *click* on the Checkout button to open the checkout page where you can pay with ApplePay or PayPal.

Install Plugins

Remember, selecting a Plugin on the vcvrack.com website doesn't download the plugin. Here are the steps and the functionality about the downloads:

- ☑ **Account - Website**: Once you are logged in to your account on the vcvrack.com website, you can only add your preferred plugins on the vcvrack.com website if you are logged in to a registered account. That means, all those plugins are linked to that specific account.

- ☑ **Account - Rack Software**: You can use the Rack software without being logged in to an existing account, however, in order to download the plugins that have been selected under a specific account, you have to log in to that account using the **Log in** ❶ button in the upper right corner of the Rack toolbar.

- ☑ **Download Plugins**: Once you logged in to your account in the Rack software, you *click* on the **Update plugins** ❷ button in the Toolbar. This will initiate the download of all the plugins that you have selected on the vcvrack.com website, but haven't downloaded yet. A progress bar ❸ appears, indicating what plugins are currently downloaded.

- ☑ **Relaunch Rack**: Once the download is complete, an Alert Dialog ❹ pops up asking you to re-launch Rack. Here is the reason why. During the download, only zip files ❺ of the selected plugins are download and placed in the folder *~/Documents/Rack/ plugins/*. The next time you launch Rack ❻, it will unzip those files to folders ❼ so they are available in the Rack software.

- ☑ **Online monitoring**: Once you are logged in to your account in the Rack software, it checks the plugins in your vcvrack account and if there are missing plugins or updated plugins, then the **Update plugins** button will have a red dot. It alerts you to click that button and download the up-to-date plugins.

- ☑ **Manage/Delete Plugins**: If you want to remove a plugin, you can disable it on the plugin page of the vcvrack.com site under your account. However, this will only stop monitoring that Plugin. You have to manually remove the Plugin folder from the *~/Documents/Rack/plugins/* directory.

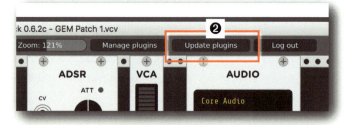

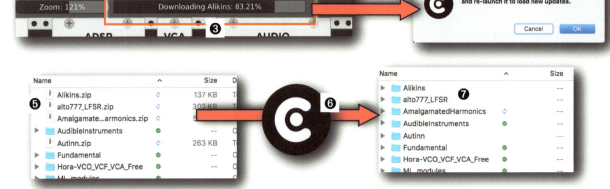

User Interface

The Rack user interface is pretty simple with a single window. On top is the Toolbar with the various buttons and controls and below is one or multiple rows of rack space where you place the synth modules.

Toolbar

➡️ *Nine Buttons*

Some of the nine buttons ❶ have a Key Command:

New Patch (*cmd+N*): This will remove all the current Modules and Patches and starts with a blank Rack space. A Dialog lets you confirm this action.

- If you want a default Patch open instead of a blank Patch, store that Patch with the name **template.vcv** and place it into the Rack directory *~/Documents/template.vcv*

Open Patch (*cmd+O*): This command will pop up an Open Dialog window, displaying the default location for the stored Patch Files *~/Documents/Rack/patches/* or the location that you recently used.

Save Patch (*cmd+S*): This command will save the current Patch to the currently open Patch. If the Patch hasn't been saved yet, then it opens the Save Dialog window, displaying the default location for the stored Patch Files *~/Documents/Rack/patches/* or the location that you recently used.

Save Patch as (*sh+cmd+N*): This command will open the Save Dialog window, displaying the default location for the stored Patch Files *~/Documents/Rack/patches/*, allowing you to save the current Patch under a different name and continue with that Patch.

Revert Patch: This command will undo all the changes you made since the last time you saved the Patch.

Disconnect Cables: Removes all the cables from the current modules.

Engine Sample Rate: Opens a popup menu ❷ where you can select the internal Sample Rate of the software (called the Engine Sample Rate), which is independent of the Sample Rate of the currently selected Audio Interface.

Toggle Power Meter: This command will open small windows ❸ beneath each module, displaying the latency of those modules.

Lock Modules: If enabled, you cannot move any existing module on the Rack. You still can add/remove modules and adjust their controls and patches. As of 0.6.2c, there is no visual indication when lock is enabled/disabled.

About the Power Meter (https://vcvrack.com/manual/Toolbar.html)

When power meters are enabled, Rack measures the amount of time spent processing each module in mS (millisamples). This is a unit of time equal to 0.001/sample rate. In many ways, this is analogous to the module power limit imposed by hardware modular synthesizers in mA (milliamperes).

To maintain a stable audio clock, the total amount of time spent processing all modules must equal 1000 mS. To achieve this, the Audio module from Core uses your audio device's high-precision clock to regulate Rack's engine, so it idles for the remaining mS until this total is met. If the Audio idle time falls close to an average of 0 mS over its block size, an audio stutter may occur. This can be caused by other modules consuming lots of mS.

Three Sliders

These three areas function as sliders when *dragging* them left-right.

- **Cable opacity ❶**: Change the opacity ("see-through") of the Cables in your current Patch. 100% ❷ not dimmed to 0% fully dimmed (invisible). Please note that even when you dimmed the cables or made them completely invisible, you still can move the mouse cursor ❸ over a jack and the Patch Cable for that specific connection is displayed.
- **Cable tension ❹**: Change the tension of the cables between "0" (hanging loose, curved ❺) and "1" (straight line ❻).
- **Zoom ❼**: Slide between 25% ❽ and 200% ❾ zoom factor depending on how many modules on the rack space you want to see inside the Rack window. The Scroll Bars appear automatically when you are zoomed in too much and not all modules can be shown inside the Rack window.

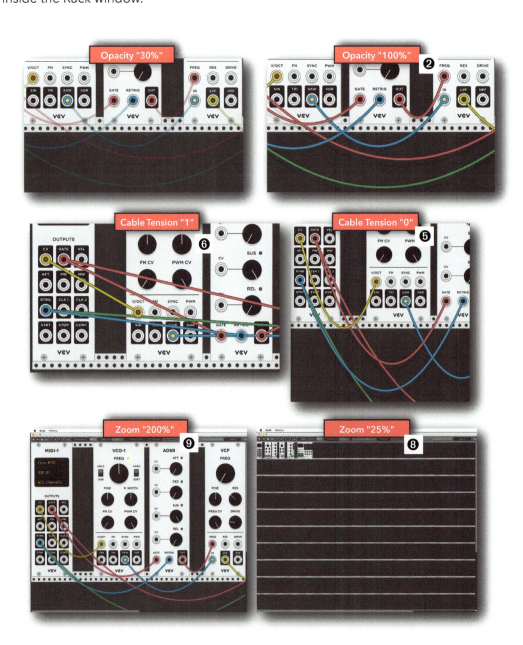

10   User Interface

➡️ *Login to your Account*

The controls to the right of the Toolbar change depending on whether you are logged in to your account or not:

❶ Register | **❷ Email** | **❸ Password** | **❹ Log in**

🟡 Not Logged In

You don't have to be logged in to an account to use Rack. However, logging in to your account lets you manage the Plugins that you downloaded for that account:

- ▶ **Register ❶**: *Click* on this button to open the vcvrack.com website to sign up for an account
- ▶ **Email ❷**: Enter the Email for the account you want to log in
- ▶ **Password ❸**: Enter the Password for the account you want to log in
- ▶ **Logic In ❹**: *Click* on this button to log in to the account with the Email/Password that you entered

🟡 Logged In

Once you logged in to your Rack account, the buttons in this area change to the following three buttons:

❺ Manage plugins | **❽ Update plugins** | **❿ Log out**

❾ Update plugins

- ▶ **Manage plugins ❺**: *Click* on this button to open the www.vcvrack.com website ❻ to download more plugins/modules. The downloaded Plugins are stored in the **plugins** folder ❼ inside the Rack folder (*~/Documents/Rack/plugins/*) inside a subfolder named after the developer.
- ▶ **Update plugins ❽**: *Click* on this button to download any new or updated Plugins that you have added to your account. A red dot ❾ indicates that there are new/updated plugins available.
- ▶ **Log out ❿**: Log out of your Rack account.

Remember:

You can only use the basic Modules that are automatically downloaded when you install the Rack software without creating an account.

However, when creating a free account you can download additional Modules (called Plugins), available by third-party developers that create modules for the Rack software.

There are two types of Plugins available, depending on the complexity of the individual Modules

- ☑️ **Free Plugins**: There are close to 100 free Plugins (often containing multiple modules for each plugin) available that you can download and use with the Rack software.
- ☑️ **Premium Plugins**: There are about 30 Modules available that you can purchase in the price range from $5 to $30.

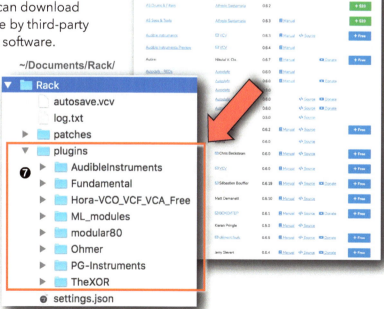

~/Documents/Rack/

Rack Space

The main user interface element of the Rack software is the rack space where you place the individual Modules, similar to a modular synth like the Eurorack.

The visible rack space depends on the following factors:

- ☑ **Window Size**: The bigger your computer screen and the size of the Rack window, the more rack space will be visible.
- ☑ **Zoom Level**: The **Zoom** slider lets you adjust the size of the Modules.
- ☑ **Vertical/Horizontal Scroll Bars**: When you zoomed in, then the vertical and horizontal scrollbars will be visible on the side of the window.

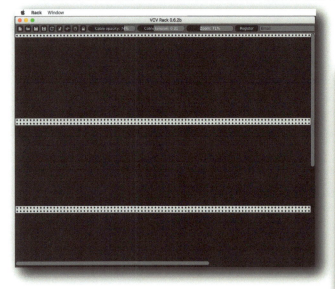

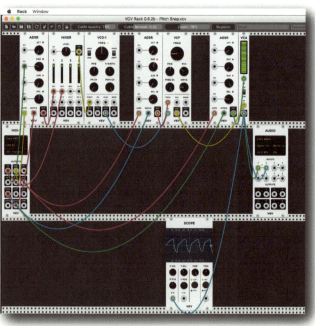

Operation

Basic Functionality

Overview

The Rack software is pretty easy to use with just a few interface elements:

🟡 Rack Window

The Rack software has only a single Main Window ❶ that represents the rack space where you place the Modules ❷, edit the Modules and connect ❸ the Modules via virtual cables (Patch Cables).

🟡 Add Modules Dialog

The Add Modules Dialog ❹ lists all the Modules that are available on your computer (currently downloaded) to be placed on the rack. *Right-click* (*ctr-click*) on the empty Rack or press the *enter* key to open that window and make a selection. The new Module will be placed at the current mouse cursor position.

🟡 Edit Modules Contextual Menu

Right-click (*ctr-click*) on a Module ❺ to open this Contextual Menu ❻ with various commands that affect that specific Module you clicked on. Some commands are also available as key commands. Some popup windows (i.e. MIDI Module) have additional commands ❼.

🟡 Toolbar

The Toolbar ❽ on top of the Rack window provides general commands. Some commands are also available as key commands.

🟡 Click-Drag Operations

All other operations are performed with the mouse. For example:

- ☑ **Click** or **drag** on the controls of a Module to set those parameter values.
- ☑ **Drag** a Module to re-position it on the Rack.
- ☑ **Drag** between Input Jacks and Output Jacks to connect them with virtual Patch Cables ❸.
- ☑ Click on a jack to trigger a control signal (i.e. **Out** on an ADSR or **EXT CLK** on a Sequencer).

Add/Remove Modules

You add a Module to your rack space from a Dialog ❶ that opens with any of the following commands:

 Right+click (*ctr+click*) on the empty rack space to place a new Module at that click position.

 Press the *enter* key on your keyboard to place a new Module at the current mouse cursor position.

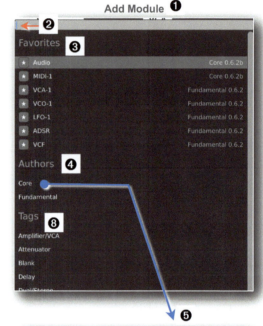

Add Module ❶

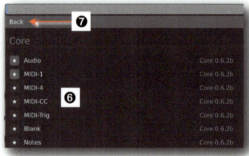

➡️ *Add Modules*

The Dialog window that opens has four sections:

🟡 *Search Field* ❷

On top of the window is a gray bar that can be easily overlooked. It is an active Search Field. Typing any text will restrict the displayed content of the window to those items that match the search string. This is an "online" search, that means it updates the displayed results as you type.

🟡 *Favorites* ❸

Any Module listed on the window has a star button that you can toggle by *clicking* on it (disabled ★, enabled ★). A Module that has this **Favorites** button enabled, will be displayed on top of this Dialog window in this **Favorites** section for easy access.
Click on any listed Module in this section to load that Module.

🟡 *Authors* ❹

This section lists the name of the developer of the Modules that you have downloaded under your account. Each item acts as a group and you *click* on an item to switch to the next window ❺ that displays all the Modules ❻ in that group. On that second window, you can *click* on a Module to load it or *click* the **Back** ❼ button to switch back to the previous window ❶.
Core and **Fundamental** are the default groups that are available after you've installed the Rack software.

🟡 *Tags* ❽

This section lets you select Modules by specific categories. *Click* on a tag to switch to the next window that displays all the Modules in that category where you can *click* on a Module to load it. Or, *click* the **Back** button to switch back to the previous window.

➡️ *Remove Module*

To remove a Module from the Rack, you can use any of the following commands:

 Click on the Module and press the *delete* key on your keyboard (please note that currently there is no visual indication whether a Module is selected or not).

 Right+click on the Module and select the **Delete** command from the Contextual Menu that pops up.

➡️ *Re-arrange Modules*

You can re-arrange the Modules on your Rack by simply *dragging* them around on the rack space.

Add/Remove Patch Cables

Like with any other electronic equipment, when you make a connection, you connect an output to an input to establish a basic signal flow. With a modular synth, that means you are using Patch Cables to make connections from an Output Jack to an Input Jack so the signal (Audio Signal or Control Signal) "flows" from the output of one Module to the input of another Module. Here is how it works with the Rack software:

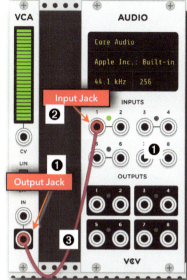

▶ **Output Jack ❶**: An Output Jack is indicated by a black background.
▶ **Input Jack ❷**: An Input Jack is indicated by a white background.
▶ **Patch/Connection ❸**: A connection is displayed by a colored Patch Cable and the jack, the cable is connected to, is changing to that same color. Remember that you can adjust the opacity and the tension of those Patch Cables.

➡ Make a Connection

Click-hold on an Output Jack (a colored Patch Cable appears) and *drag* it over to an Input Jack. The Patch Cable between the two jacks is now visible.

Please note that you cannot drag a connection to an Input Jack that is already used by a different Patch Cable, already receiving an output signal.

➡ Patch Cable Color

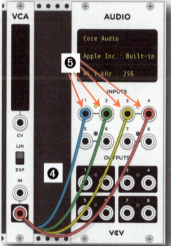

There are four available colors ❹ for the Patch Cables (red, green, blue, yellow). *Click-hold* on a jack (before dragging the cable over the next jack) and you see the color for that cable. If you want a different color, release the mouse and *click-hold* again on the jack to get the next color, and again until the color you want appears. It is like cycling through the four color choices.

➡ Color Indications

Please pay close attention to the colors on your Rack because there are small but useful indications that help you keep track of your Patch, especially if it grows more complex.

☑ **Patch Cables**: The Patch Cable always has one of the four colors ❹, the one you chose when you make the connection. To change to a different color, you have to remove the connection and drag a new connection with the proper color.

☑ **Jack Ring**: Once a jack is connected, the ring ❺ of that Jack also adapts to the color of the Patch Cable. This colored ring is visible even if you hide ❻ the Patch Cables (Opacity 0%). I always recommend to use a specific color code, for example, blue for Audio Signal, red for Control Signals, yellow for Clock Signals, then it becomes much easier to follow a complex Patch with lots of connections.

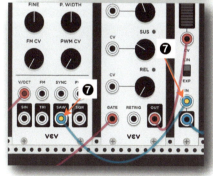

☑ **Jack Center**: The center ❼ of a jack illuminates whenever there is a signal passing through the jack. Another useful feedback when monitoring and troubleshooting a Patch.

➡️ Make one-to-many Connections

To patch an output ❶ to multiple inputs ❷ (Y-cable), you don't have to use a Multiplier Module. You have two easy options to do that, for example, when patching the output of the VCA Module ❸ to the left and right input of the Audio Module (the Audio Interface ❹:

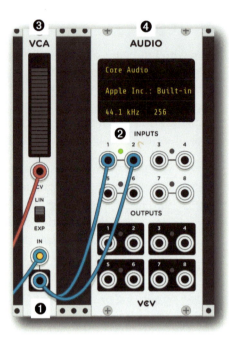

- 📌 Hold down the **cmd** key before *dragging* an additional connection from an Output Jack that has already a connection.
- 📌 *Drag* the connection in the opposite direction, from the Input Jack to the Output Jack.

➡️ Change Connection

Changing an existing connection

- 📌 *Click* on any Input Jack or Output Jack a Patch Cable is connected to and *drag* it to a different jack.
- 📌 With an Output Jack that is connected to multiple Input Jacks, it is easier to *drag* the cable at the end of the Output Jack.

➡️ Remove Single Connection

There are two procedures on how to remove a single Patch Cable. Don't use them on an Output Jack that is patched to multiple Input Jacks:

- 📌 *Ctr+click* on the Input Jack or Output Jack the Patch Cable is connected to.
- 📌 *Drag* the Patch Cable away from the Input Jack or Output Jack and release the mouse.

➡️ Remove All Connections on a Module

To remove all the connections, all Patch Cables, on a specific Module, you *click* on the Module and choose any of the two options:

- 📌 *Right-click* (or *ctr+click*) on the Module and select the command **Disconnect cables** from the Contextual Menu ❺.
- 📌 *Click* on the Module (please note that in v0.6.2c there is no visual indication whether a Module is selected or not) and use the key command **cmd+U**.

➡️ Remove All Connections on the Rack

To remove all connections, all Patch Cables on your rack, *click* on the "cat" button 🐱 in the Toolbar ❻. An Alert Dialog ❼ opens to confirm this action (that you cannot undo).

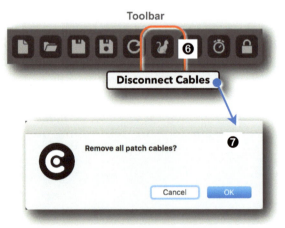

Toolbar

Configure Modules

When you *right-click* (*ctr+click*) on a Module, a Contextual Menu ❶ opens with various commands that apply to that Module:

▶ **Initialize** (*cmd+I*): This command resets all parameters/controls on that Module to their default values.

▶ **Randomize** (*cmd+R*): Every time you choose this command, the values for the available parameters on that Module are set to a random value.

▶ **Disconnect cables** (*cmd+U*): This command removes all connections (Patch Cables) on the Module.

▶ **Duplicate** (*cmd+D*): This command loads that same Module with the current settings to the next available position on the Rack. Connections on the Module are not copied.

Presets

A Preset is like a snapshot of the current value of all parameters on a specific Module.

You can copy/paste Presets between Modules on a Rack (of course, only between identical Modules) and also **Save** Presets to a Preset File and later **Load** Preset from a Preset File.

All those commands are available from the popup menu ❶ when you *right-click* (*ctr+click*) on a Module. Some commands are available as key commands.

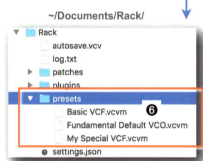

➡️ *Copy/Paste*

▶ **Copy preset** (*cmd+C*): This command copies the Preset to the clipboard.

▶ **Paste preset** (*cmd+V*): This command pastes the Preset that was previously copied to the clipboard onto that Module, overwriting its current values.

➡️ *Preset Files*

There are two commands that are only available from the Contextual Menu:

🟡 *Save Preset*

Selecting the **Save preset** ❷ command opens the Save Dialog ❸ with the **presets** ❹ folder selected. This is the folder inside the **Rack** folder (*~/Documents/Rack/*). Enter a name and click **Save** ❺. Two things to pay attention to:

▶ The Preset File has the **.vcvm** file extension ❻ but no indication for what Module that Preset is for. Therefore, you have to give the Preset File a name that indicates the Module that Preset is for.

▶ You can save the Preset File to any other location and even exchange Presets with other users.

🟡 *Load Preset*

Selecting the **Load preset** command opens the Open Dialog with the **presets** folder selected. Select any Preset to load it or navigate to any other folder where you have stored your Presets.

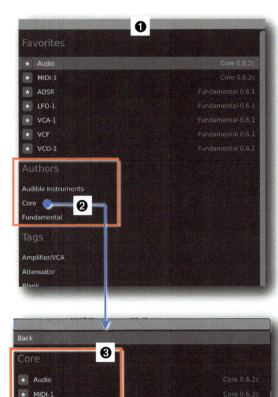

Core Modules

The Add Modules Dialog ❶ that lets you load Modules has a special default category under the **Authors** section called "**Core**" ❷. In addition to a Notes Module (that lets you enter some text) and the Blank Module (a blank faceplate), it contains ❸ the Modules that let you configure how the Rack software (your specific Patch) interacts with MIDI Signals and Audio Signals on your computer.

Please note that the Core Modules are not stored in the *~/Documents/Rack/Plugins/* directory with all the other Plugins. They are stored inside the actually Rack application.

More info about the Core Modules at

https://vcvrack.com/manual/Core.html

Blank

Loading the Blank Module ❹ adds exactly that, a blank module, just like on a hardware rack to fill any gaps between modules and make it look more nicer.

Once you have placed the Blank Module on the rack space, you can *drag* its left or right border to resize its width. The minimum width is 3 HP (Horizontal Pitch).

Notes

Loading the Notes Module ❺ adds a Module with a big text area. *Click* on it to place the blue insertion cursor there, and you can enter any text, i.e., notes or instructions about the Patch.

Audio

The Audio Module ❹ lets you configure which Audio Interface you use to route the Audio Signal from and to your Rack Modules. This is a similar setting found in any DAW where you choose the Audio Interface (the Audio Device) it uses.

The Audio Module has four settings. *Click* on the corresponding text field on top to open its popup menu with the available options.

- **⬤ Driver ❶**
  - ☑ **Core Audio ❷**: Select this option to play the audio of your Patch directly to any of the available Audio Interfaces (Core Audio is the built-in audio driver in macOS).
  - ☑ **Bridge ❸**: Select this option when you want to use your Patch "inside" your DAW, for example, Logic Pro X.
- **⬤ Audio Interface (Device) ❹**: The available options in this menu depend on what driver is selected in the first field.
  - ☑ **Core Audio**: The menu ❺ displays all the Audio Interfaces that are available in macOS. Choose the one you want to use as the audio output for your Patch.
  - ☑ **Bridge**: The menu ❻ displays a list of 16 Ports that you use to route the audio signal. The "VCV Bridge" Plugin that you use in your DAW to receive the audio signal from the Patch has to be set to that same port.

- **⬤ Sample Rate ❼**:
  Click on this section to set the Sample Rate for the selected Audio Interface. The option (**Locked by device**) ❽ is displayed if the currently selected audio interface won't allow any Sample Rate changes.

- **⬤ Buffer Size ❾**:
  Click on this section to set the Buffer Size that affects the latency similar to DAW settings. The option (**Locked by device**) ❿ is displayed if the currently selected audio interface won't allow any Buffer Size changes.

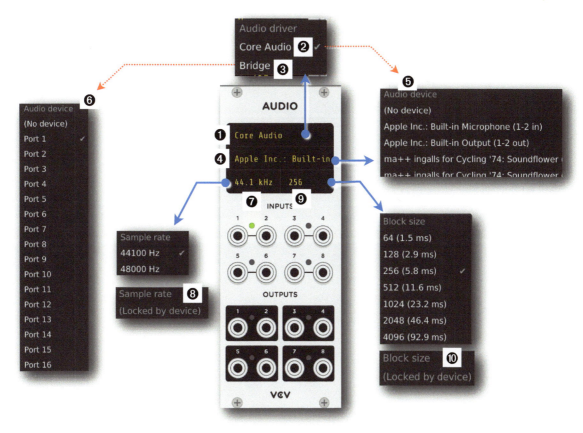

MIDI

Usually, with modular synths, you have a musical keyboard that produces a CV Gate and CV Pitch output. Modular systems also might have a MIDI Module that converts MIDI signals into those CV signals. The available MIDI Modules in the **Core** category have the same functionality. The different Modules have different capabilities regarding the MIDI conversion. More details about the individual functions can be found at the vcvrack website https://vcvrack.com/manual/Core.html.

Here is the basic functionality about the three fields that let you set up the MIDI Module:

● **MIDI Driver ❶**: The popup menu lets you select any of the four drivers. The selection determines what options are available in the second field below.

  ▶ **Core MIDI ❷**: Select **Core MIDI** if you want to route any of the MIDI keyboards connected to your computer to that Module.

  ▶ **Bridge ❸**: Use this option when using Rack "inside" a DAW as a plugin

  ▶ **Computer keyboard ❹**: This is a useful option if you don't have any external MIDI keyboard available. You can use the keys on your computer keyboard (QWERTY keyboard) as a musical keyboard.

  ▶ **Gamepad ❺**: To use a connected Game Controller as an input device.

● **MIDI Device ❻**: The available options in this menu depend on what driver is selected in the first field. If you selected Core MIDI, *click* on this section to open a popup menu with all the MIDI Interfaces ❼ available on your computer. Select the MIDI Keyboard/Controller that you want to use to play the Rack.

● **MIDI Channels ❽**: Select the incoming MIDI Channel that you want to use as the MIDI input, or leave it at "**All Channels**" to allow MIDI Messages transmitting on any MIDI Channel to reach the Rack Module.

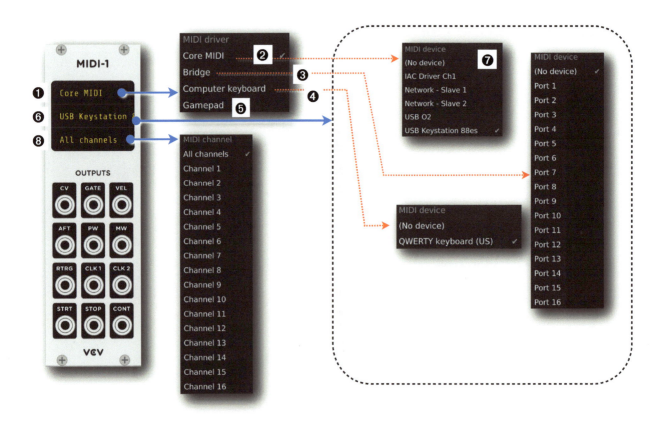

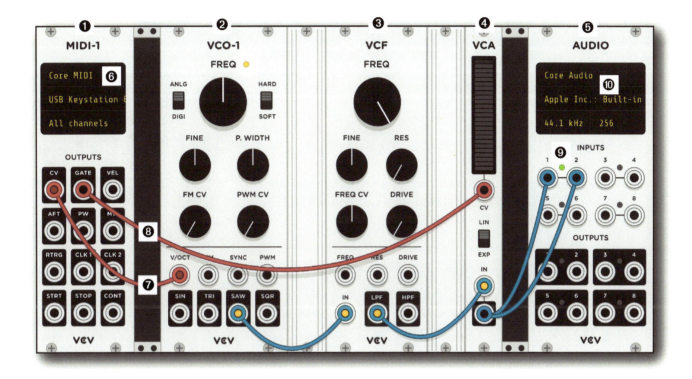

Basic Patch

Here is a basic Patch with the MIDI Module and Audio Module used with the three main components (VCO, VCF, VCA) of a modular synth.

 MIDI ❶

In this example, the MIDI Module uses the CoreMIDI driver ❻ of macOS and uses the USB Keystation 88 keyboard controller connected to the computer as the MIDI Keyboard that can play the Rack.
The CV Pitch ❼ output from that Module is patched to the **1V/Oct** CV Input of the VCO, and the CV Gate ❽ output is patched to the **CV** Gate Input of the VCA.

 VCO ❷

The VCO receives the CV Pitch on its 1V/Oct jack to control the pitch. Its Sawtooth waveform output (Audio Signal) is patched to the VCF Audio Input.

 VCF ❸

The VCA receives the Audio Signal from the VCO and sends its Audio Signal from the **LPF** out (Low Pass Filter) to the VCA Audio Input.

➡ **VCA ❹**

The VCA receives the CV Gate signal ❽ from the MIDI Module to control the note on/off and receives the Audio Signal on its input, coming from the VCF. The Audio Signal is sent from its Output Jack to the Audio Module.

➡ **Audio ❺**

The Audio Signal from the VCA is patched to the input 1 and input 2 ❾ of the Audio Module to route the mono signal to the left and right channel of the Audio Interface ❿ that is selected in the Audio Module. In this example, it is the Built-in output of the computer.

Standalone vs. Plugin

Rack in Standalone Mode

This is the basic operation where the Rack software acts as a standalone software application:

- ☑ **MIDI**: The MIDI Module ❶ is configured to receive MIDI data directly from any external MIDI controller ❷ that is available on the computer.
- ☑ **Audio**: The Audio Module ❸ is configured to send the audio signal the Rack is producing directly to any of the available Audio Interfaces ❹ on the computer.

Rack in Bridge Mode

This operation allow any DAW to use the Rack application "internally" as a virtual Plugin, although it operates "externally" as a separate software application.

- ☑ **Bridge Plugin**: The Bridge Plugin ❺ is part of the VCV Rack installation. Once installed, it can be opened in the DAW like any other third-party Plugin (AU standard or VST standard). The Plugin functions as a "handshake" between the DAW and the Rack software to exchange the MIDI and Audio data between the two.
- ☑ **MIDI**: The MIDI Controller ❻ is connected to the DAW as usual, where its MIDI data is recorded ❼ on the selected Instrument Track. If the Bridge Plugin ❺ is loaded on such a Track, then that MIDI data on that Track is played on (sent to) the Rack application ❽.

- ☑ **Audio**: Any audio on the DAW is played through the selected Audio Interface ❾. If the Bridge Plugin ❺ is loaded on such an Audio Track, then any Audio Signal from the Rack software ❿ is received by the DAW (through the Bridge Plugin) and can be mixed and played back as part of the DAW Project.
- ☑ **MIDI Clock**: Another advantage of the VCV Bridge Plugin is that it can also send MIDI Clock to the Rack application to sync, for example, a Sequencer Module that is used in a Rack Patch.

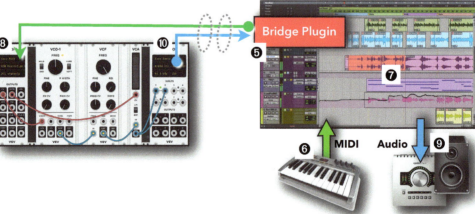

The explanation of the VCV Bridge Plugin on the previous page describes the basic concept. However, the actual implementation is slightly different in various DAWs.

3-Step Configuration for Logic Pro X

The configuration for using the Rack software as a Plugin in Logic requires three steps.

➡ Step 1 - IAC Driver Configuration

Logic doesn't use the VCV Bridge Plugin to send its MIDI data to the Rack application. Instead, it uses the IAC Driver, a built-in MIDI Device that is part of macOS.

"Audio MIDI Setup" utility app

⬤ About the IAC Driver

Here are some facts about the IAC Driver:

▶ IAC is an acronym for "Inter-Application Communication"

▶ The IAC is a protocol in macOS, providing virtual MIDI cables that let you route MIDI Messages between applications.

▶ The individual applications don't have to support that protocol or even know about it, because macOS provides a special MIDI Device called "**IAC Driver**" and any application on the Mac that supports MIDI (CoreAudio compliant) sees that Device like any other connected MIDI Device.

▶ The IAC Driver is available in the **Audio MIDI Setup ❶** utility app along with any other MIDI Device available on your computer, for example, all the external MIDI keyboards and MIDI controllers connected to your computer.

▶ Open the Audio MIDI Setup utility app, located in the **/Applications/Utilities/** directory, and open the **MIDI Studio** window ❷ (**cmd+2**).

▶ By default, the IAC Driver has one Bus (virtual MIDI Bus), but you can add additional busses to that driver (MIDI Device) to create multiple "pipelines" to transfer MIDI data between applications. **Double-click** on the IAC Driver icon ❸ to open its configuration window for that.

▶ Once configured, you choose one of the Busses of the IAC Device on the application that is sending the MIDI data, and you select the same IAC Bus on the application that is receiving the MIDI data. This establishes the virtual MIDI Bus between those applications.

⬤ IAC Driver Configuration

The good news is that you don't even have to open the Audio MIDI Setup application, because the IAC Driver exists by default and its default configuration with a single Bus is all you need for using the Rack application in Bridge Mode with Logic Pro X.

Step 2 - Rack Configuration

Now, on the Rack software, you have to configure two things for the basic setup, the MIDI Module ❶ and the Audio Module ❷.

🟡 MIDI Module

Once you add the MIDI Module to your Patch, you have to set the three fields the following way:

▶ **MIDI Driver**: ❸ *Click* on the first field and select Core MIDI, because the IAC Driver is part of the macOS CoreMIDI architecture.

▶ **MIDI Device** ❹: *Click* on the second field to open the popup menu that shows all the available MIDI Devices on your computer. One option should be the "**IAC Driver IAC Bus 1**" ❺. This represents Bus 1 of the IAC Device. By selecting this option, the Rack software receives MIDI Messages from any application that is sending its MIDI Messages over that same IAC Bus 1 (which will be Logic Pro X as we will see on the next page)

▶ **MIDI Channel** ❻: Like with any physical MIDI cable, the virtual MIDI cable of an IAC Bus also has 16 MIDI Channels. You can leave this option at its default setting "**All channels**" to receive MIDI messages regardless of what MIDI Channel they belong to.

🟡 Audio Module

On the Audio Module, you have to choose the following options:

▶ **Audio Driver** ❼: *Click* on the first field and select **Bridge** ❽. That means the Rack application is sending its audio not to any of the available audio interfaces, but to the DAW application that uses the VCV Bridge Plugin on a specific Track. This functions like a virtual audio cable that sends the audio signal internally from the Rack application to the DAW application (in our case, Logic Pro X).

▶ **Port** ❾: Once the Bridge Driver is selected in the first field, then the second field is automatically set to Port 1. If you *click* on the field, a popup menu opens that lets you select any of the 16 Ports ❿. This is useful if you have multiple Audio Modules in your Rack setup that route the audio to separate VCV Bridge Plugins. As we will see, the VCV Bridge Plugin can also be set to any of the 16 Ports to determine from which Audio Module a Plugin is receiving its audio signals from.

➡️ *Step 3 - Logic Pro X Configuration*

Now to the final configuration step, Logic Pro X. Logic has a very elegant solution that makes it possible to use only one Track for sending the MIDI signal and receiving the audio signal, similar to a Software Instrument Track. No extra Aux Track as a return is required.

🟡 *Instrument Channel Strip*

First, create a new Software Instrument Track ❶. That is the Track that provides the two functions, recording the MIDI notes as MIDI Regions ❷ (that are sent to the Rack application) and receive the audio signal back from the Rack software.

🟡 *External Instrument Plugin*

On the Instrument Slot ❸ of the Software Instrument Channel Strip you don't select any of the Instrument Plugins; instead, you choose the special Plugin "**External Instrument**". It is a little bit hidden. *Click* on the Instrument Slot of the Channel Strip and scroll down to the **Utility** ❹ folder. One of the three Plugins inside that folder is the **External Instrument** Plugin ❺. You can choose Stereo or Mono, depending on how you set up your Patch in the Rack application. Once the Plugin is loaded, *click* the blue button ❸ to open the Plugin Window ❻ to configure it. This Plugin is used for integrating external hardware MIDI Sound Modules ❼ in your Logic Project by sending the MIDI Messages to the MIDI Device the Sound Module is connected to (**MIDI Destination ❽**) and selecting the Audio Input where the audio out of the Sound Module is connected to (**Input ❾**).

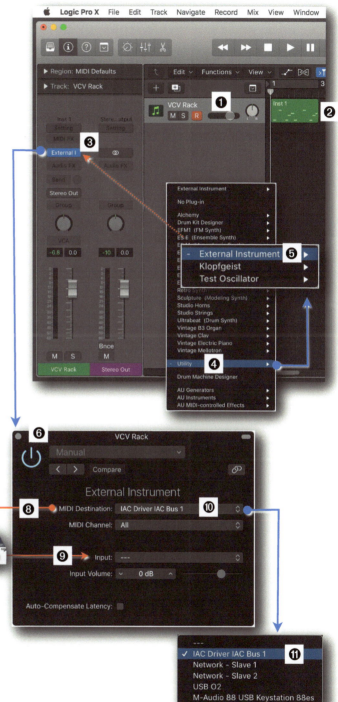

> ▶ **MIDI Destination**: When you *click* on the MIDI Destination Selector ❿, you will see all the MIDI Devices in the popup menu that are available on your computer. And as you can see, we also have the **IAC Driver IAC Bus 1** ⓫ option, and that is exactly what to select. That means any MIDI Messages on that Track, either when playing back a MIDI Region ❷ on the Track or playing that Track live when the Track is selected ❶, will be routed to the MIDI Module on the Rack application via this internal virtual IAC MIDI cable

> ▶ **Input**: The Input ❾ is usually the place where you select a channel of the external Audio Interface so the audio signal of the external MIDI Sound Module is routed back into the Software Instrument Channel Strip. However, the audio signal of the Rack software (that functions as the MIDI Sound Module in our case) won't "come back" on the audio interface. That's why we can ignore that menu and, instead, configure the audio return in the next section.

🟡 *VCV Bridge Plugin*

Now that we established the virtual pipeline to route MIDI Messages from the Software Instrument Track in Logic to the MIDI Module in the Rack application, we have to establish the second pipeline, to route the audio from the Audio Module of the Rack application back to the Software Instrument Track where the MIDI was coming from. And for that, we use the VCV Bridge Plugin that you hopefully had installed when you downloaded the Rack software (see the chapter at the beginning of the book).

▶ **Load Plugin:** *Click* on the first Audio FX Slot ❶ on the Software Instrument Channel Strip that opens the Plugin Menu ❷, scroll all the way down to the **Audio Units** ❸ folder and in that submenu you should see the menu item **VCV** ❹, a folder that contains the **VCV Bridge** ❺ Plugin. Select it (mono or stereo, depending on your Rack Patch) to load that Plugin.

▶ **Select Port:** Once the VCV Bridge Plugin is loaded on the first Audio FX Slot, *click* on that Plugin Button to open its Plugin Window ❻. The first selector, labeled **Port** ❼, opens a popup menu where you can select the Port 1 to 16. Because we set the Audio Module on the Rack application to Port 1, we also have to set the Plugin to Port 1 ❽, so it receives the audio signal from the Rack software.

About the Audio FX Plugin

In case you are interested in how that audio routing works regarding the Audio FX Plugin:

- Usually, the Audio FX Plugin on the first Audio FX Plugin Slot in Logic receives its audio input from the audio output of the Software Instrument Plugin on that Channel Strip.
- The audio output of the first Audio FX Plugin is then sent to the audio input of the Audio FX Plugin on the next Audio FX Slot and so on until the Audio FX Plugin on the last slot sends its audio signal to the Volume Fader and then to the Pan Control.
- The VCV Bridge Plugin, however, is special because it uses a virtual audio input, the audio signal that is routed internally through the VCV Bridge Port mechanism, like a secret (audio) back door into Logic.
- By placing the VCV Bridge Plugin on an Audio FX Slot, any audio signal from the Instrument Plugin or a previous Audio FX Plugin (if the VCV Bridge Plugin is placed on a slot other than slot 1) is interrupted and the incoming audio signal (through its back door) has priority.
- That is the reason why on the External Instrument Plugin (that we configured in step 2) we don't have to specify an Audio Input (a return).

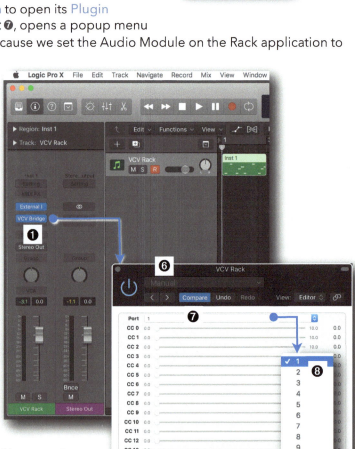

Here are two additional functionalities when using the Bridge Plugin in Logic Pro X:

➡️ *Record Audio*

If you adjust controls on the Rack while playing and want to record that as audio into your Logic Project, do the following.

- ☑️ On the Software Instrument Channel Strip that we just configured, you change the Output Routing to a bus ❶ (i.e., Bus 1).
- ☑️ You create a new Audio Track ❷, and on its Input Slot ❸, you select **Bus 1** as its input to route the audio from the Instrument Channel Strip ❶ to that Audio Channel Strip ❷.
- ☑️ Now, while you are playing back the Project, you record the audio from the Rack application on that Audio Track.

➡️ *Synchronize Rack Sequencer*

Another world of new opportunities opens up when you sync the Rack Patch via MIDI Clock to your Logic Project. Here is an example of a basic setup.

🟡 *Enable MIDI Clock (Logic Pro X)*

In Logic Pro X, select from the menu *File ➤ Project Settings ➤ Synchronization...* to go to the Synchronization ❹ window and *click* the MIDI ❺ tab.

- ☑️ **Enable MIDI Clock**: Next to the **Transmit to:** label, enable the **Destination 1** ❻ checkbox
- ☑️ **Choose Destination**: *Click* the selector below and choose from the popup menu what MIDI Device you are sending the MIDI Clock to. In our case, you select **IAC Driver IAC Bus 1** ❼ again to send the MIDI Clock to the MIDI Module ❽ in our Rack Patch.

🟡 *Patch MIDI Clock (Rack)*

On the MIDI Module ❽ of the Rack Patch, you connect the **CLK** ❾ Output Jack (that is where the MIDI Clock from Logic Pro X "arrives") to the **EXT Clock** ❿ Input Jack of the Sequencer Module. Now when you enable the Run button on the Sequencer Module, the Sequencer only starts when it receives a MIDI Clock signal from Logic (that means whenever you play back Logic).

Please note that when you *right+click* on the MIDI Module, the Contextual Menu will have two Clock Rate options to set the relationship between the Sequencer Steps and the MIDI Clock.

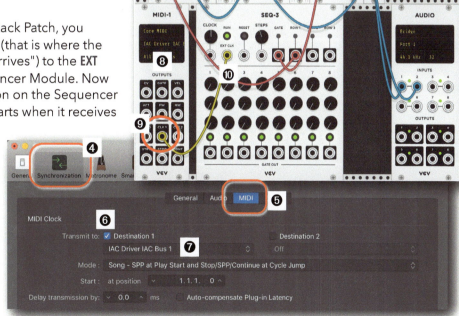

Conclusion

This concludes my manual *"VCV Rack -How it Works"*.

If you find my visual approach to explaining features and concepts helpful, please recommend my books to others or maybe write a review on Amazon or the iBooks Store. This will help me to continue this series.
To check out other books in my "Graphically Enhanced Manuals" series, go to my website at:
www.DingDingMusic.com/Manuals

To contact me directly, email me at GEM@DingDingMusic.com

More information about my day job as a composer and links to my social network sites are on my website:
www.DingDingMusic.com

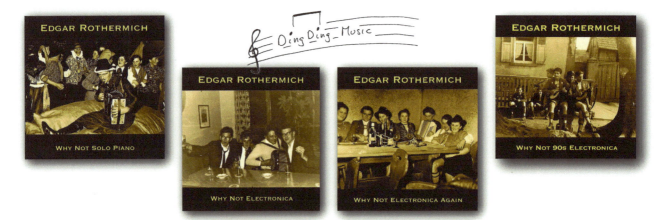

Listen to my music on SoundCloud

Thanks for your interest and your support,

Edgar Rothermich

www.ingramcontent.com/pod-product-compliance
Lightning Source LLC
Chambersburg PA
CBHW041433050326
40690CB00002B/534